A Child's Story of Jesus

written by Barbara Kanaar

illustrated by Kathryn Hutton

Library of Congress Catalog Card No. 85-62957
© 1986. The STANDARD PUBLISHING Company, Cincinnati, Ohio
Division of STANDEX INTERNATIONAL Corporation. Printed in U.S.A.

Baby Jesus was born one night long, long ago in the town of Bethlehem. He was born in a small stable where cows and donkeys were kept. Mary and Joseph loved Baby Jesus.

Mary wrapped Baby Jesus in some soft pieces of cloth. She carefully laid Him in a little box filled with clean hay. Then Mary and Joseph thanked God for sending His Son.

Look inside the stable and find Baby Jesus sleeping in His little bed called a manger. A manger is a box that holds food for cows and donkeys. Point to all the animals inside the stable. See if you can name every one of them.

Some happy shepherds came to see Baby Jesus. They came after many singing angels told them where to find the baby. The happy shepherds thanked God for sending His Son.

Look at the picture and see if you can find: Mary and Joseph looking at Baby Jesus in His manger-bed; many shining angels in the sky; the shepherds with their sheep coming to see Baby Jesus; the bright stars in the night sky.

Can you find a star in the picture that is
bigger and brighter than all the other stars
in the sky? This beautiful star led the wise
men to Jesus' house. Can you find where
Jesus lived?

Baby Jesus had grown until He was no
longer a tiny baby but a little boy. The wise
men were happy to see the little boy, Jesus.
They gave Him many nice presents and
thanked God for sending His Son.

Mary and Joseph and Jesus lived in the little town of Nazareth. Joseph was a carpenter. A carpenter makes things out of wood. When Jesus was a boy, He helped Joseph.

Look at the picture and see if you can find Jesus and Joseph working in the carpenter shop. Point to the hammer and saw they used to make a little chair. What are some of the other things they have made from wood?

Jesus was a good helper. What are some things that you can do to help your mother and father?

When Jesus became a man, He began to tell people everywhere about His Father, God. He called some men to be His special helpers. These helpers were called disciples.

Can you count how many disciples Jesus called? One, two, three, four, five, six, seven, eight, nine, ten, eleven, twelve.

Those twelve men loved Jesus, and they were happy to help Him.

Jesus and His disciples were out on a lake during a big storm. Look at the picture and find their little boat. Point to the big, black clouds and the streaks of lightning in the dark sky.

Jesus was sleeping in the boat, and the disciples were afraid. They woke Jesus up and told Him how scared they were.

Do you see Jesus standing in the boat? He told the big storm to be quiet. Then there was no more thunder and lightning. The wind stopped blowing, and the lake was still.

The disciples knew that only God's Son could quiet such a big storm!

Can you think of a time when you were sick and couldn't go outside to play? The little girl in the picture had been very, very sick. She had to stay in bed, and this made her very unhappy. Her father and mother were unhappy too, because they thought their little girl would never be well again.

One day Jesus came to visit the little girl. Point to Jesus sitting near her bed. He told the little girl to get up, and she did! She was no longer sick! She could walk and run and jump and play. The little girl was very happy. What do you think she said to Jesus?

Find the happy father and mother standing near Jesus. They knew He was God's Son. Only God's Son could make a sick person well!

Can you find Zaccheus high in the tree? He wanted to see Jesus, but Zaccheus was a short man. He could not see over the heads of all the people.

The people did not like Zaccheus because he took their money and kept it for himself.

Jesus saw Zaccheus in the tree and told him to come down. Nobody, not even Zaccheus, could hide from Jesus.

Jesus asked Zaccheus to be His friend, and this made Zaccheus very happy. He gave back all the money he had taken. Zaccheus showed Jesus he loved Him by being kind to other people. How can you show Jesus that you love Him, too?

Do you know what was inside the basket that this little boy brought to Jesus? Yes, two little fish and five loaves of bread.

All day long many, many people had been listening to Jesus tell them about God. Now the people were hungry, but they had no food to eat.

Only this little boy had brought a lunch. Jesus took the lunch and thanked God for the food. Then He made the small lunch big so everyone had enough to eat.

Aren't you glad that this little boy shared his lunch with Jesus? And aren't you glad that Jesus cared for all those people?

One day Jesus rode into a city on a little donkey. Many happy people followed Him. They loved Jesus so much that they sang songs to Him. Some of the people laid their coats in the road for Jesus to ride over. Others waved palm branches in the air.

Look at the picture and see if you can find: Jesus riding on the donkey; a grandfather and grandmother; a happy father and mother; a boy and girl; a small, smiling baby.

It was a wonderful day for all the people. They knew Jesus loved them, and they were very happy.

It was time for Jesus to go home to Heaven. He had finished all the work God wanted Him to do.

Jesus told His disciples He would always be with them. He told them to tell people everywhere that He loved them. Then Jesus went up into the sky. Can you see Jesus going up into the clouds? Do you see the disciples watching on the ground?

Jesus went up higher and higher. Soon He was hidden in the clouds. The disciples looked and looked for Jesus but they could not see Him.

The disciples knew Jesus was in Heaven. They were so happy. What do you think they did? They told everyone they met about Jesus, God's wonderful Son.

Jesus is your special Friend. He cares for you each day and loves you very much. Jesus wants you to love Him too!

You can tell Jesus you love Him by talking to Him every day.

You can show Jesus you love Him by the things you do and say.

Aren't you thankful for God's wonderful Son, Jesus?